A Case for the Dead Letter Detective

A Case for the Dead Letter Detective

Poems by

Lori Brack

© 2021 Lori Brack. All rights reserved.
This material may not be reproduced in any form, published,
reprinted, recorded, performed, broadcast,
rewritten or redistributed without
the explicit permission of Lori Brack.
All such actions are strictly prohibited by law.

Cover design by Shay Culligan
Author photograph by Maggie Mae
Cover photograph by Lori Brack

ISBN: 978-1-952326-98-1

Kelsay Books
502 South 1040 East, A-119
American Fork, Utah, 84003

In memory of my father Richard
and for my sister Mary Jane

Acknowledgments

Mid-American Review: "The Dead Letter Detective Listens for a Sign," "A Natural History of Mail"

Packingtown Review: "The Dead Letter Detective Finds a Clue," "The Dead Letter Detective Writes to His Lover," "The Dead Letter Detective Grows Old"

Superstition Review: "Memory of the Green Office," "Detective's Lucid Dream," "A Scholar of Disorder," "Detective's Holiday"

I-70 Review: "The Dead Letter Detective as a Boy," "The Dead Letter Detective Uncovers the Address"

Contents

The Dead Letter Detective Listens for a Sign	11
Another Case for the Dead Letter Detective	12
A Scholar of Disorder	13
The Dead Letter Detective as a Boy	14
Flowering Crabapple	15
In the Book of Rare Stamps	16
Owlet, Tiger, Clearwing, Sphinx	17
A Natural History of Mail	18
What the Postmark Knows	19
Memory of the Green Office	20
Overtime for the Dead Letter Detective	21
The Brain's Letterbox	22
The Dead Letter Detective Writes to His Lover	23
The Dead Letter Detective Uncovers the Address	24
What It Means To Want	25
Detective's Holiday	26
The Dead Letter Detective in Spring	27
The Dead Letter Detective Meets His Match	28
Detective's Lucid Dream	29
His Métier	30
Deep Afternoon of the Detective	31
Into the Almost	32
The Dead Letter Detective Grows Old	33
The Dead Letter Detective Finds a Clue	34

The Dead Letter Detective Listens for a Sign

He knows the best things are hidden, each cupboard concealing what it does—cool sheets, a favorite cup, rustle of tissue paper and scent he mistakes for the fragrance of peonies. He has opened such envelopes again and again, studied the stamps, noted national beasts and currencies. Before he undoes each flap, his stethoscope investigates the inner clockwork. Plugged to his ears, cold bell of the instrument: hiss of his room, sudden breath and the roar of sighing. If he could choose which one to open, it would be the lion every time, the great furred head, its maw full of singing teeth.

Another Case for the Dead Letter Detective

You have a hole in the side of your life. Everyone who looks in sees something else. You try electrical tape over the slot, but it peels away. Someone drops his ring into the hole and someone loses her eyeglasses. You begin to jangle when you dance. One day the hole sounds better than you ever could. You tell it to pipe down.

The hole in the side of your life spits out things you didn't know were there—a lopsided merry-go-round, a lilac bush where a boy waits, a key to a mailbox you forgot you had, piling up with letters. You climb into the blossoms with the boy. He touches your elbow inside the white sweater you're wearing because it hides the hole. He talks you into taking a spin on the merry-go-round and when you are whirling, he smiles and swallows the key.

A Scholar of Disorder

Chilly dusk murmurs a 4 o'clock word. Late, and still this much to do: another letter, fitted to the paper, its ragged margins. The detective commands a magician's reputation in the halls of the dead letter branch. When some junior member is stumped, the detective is summoned to divine the address—fingerprint smudges and ghosts of lines, brown ink spilled in one corner, a blotch the shape of a bird's heart. He squints to read the name, faded as the life. He bends nearer to the page, his heart whispering in his wrists.

The Dead Letter Detective as a Boy

Each childhood discovers and then conceals. May morning—all the other boys running over grass and he, hands cupped to the glass, peers through the mausoleum grate. Sunlight through high windows filters the leafy floor. Someone's plastic roses dulled by dust. A still wasp, half wrapped in cobweb. Veined marble and ranks of bronze with names he strains to read. He rattles the big handles in his childish hands that cannot undo these doors.

Flowering Crabapple

His fingers dipped
into and out of the tree,
scrabbling for the dimestore ring
snapped inside a faded
velvet box. Dying, the tree
opened a coffer to him
where a branch dropped
away, round as a wrist.
He mailed valentines
at the tree, whispered secrets
to the dark interior, its breath
smelling of animals and rot.
Every spring until it fell, white
blossoms broke out on limbs
and starlings built nests on his treasure
but never once flew away wearing
a paper heart, a single glass jewel.

In the Book of Rare Stamps

A wingtip, a trailing
bird toe slips
              off
the stamp's perforated
edge—crenellated cage
can't keep him in

Owlet, Tiger, Clearwing, Sphinx

A white tangent catches the corner of his eye. Outside another letter falls, then a shower of rectangles spills on workers chasing mail, plucking it from shrubbery. He blinks the paper downpour out of his eyes and the very next envelope he picks up strains toward the window, flutters like life in his hand.

A Natural History of Mail

Lichen-bound, the letterbox of the long-tailed tit hangs feather lined and spider silken.

When a dormouse collects the mail, it visits an August blackberry thicket drifting with purple ink where it must elude young women's pluck and grasp.

A firefly mailbox looks overturned to the unpracticed eye, a jelly jar of twinkling code. Closer inspection brings to light a whole post office flashing late, summer, grass.

Crows aren't on the postal route. If once they could read, they have forgotten how. When too far for rasp and cackle they prefer long-distance wings and tails, feather black messages zipping through the sky over the roof he sits under right now.

What the Postmark Knows

The mailbox before the letter carrier is a humped shape on its post, flat tongue closed tab to tab. A mailbox with a little inside sounds the same: tight ripe clang, tinny pitch. Each private cubby, watertight, opens a black aperture for the delivery folded and sealed—slender packages made of paper and ink, not a rustle or squeak, keeping something or nothing to themselves.

Memory of the Green Office

The desks are green. The floors. The rank
of files against one wall and light
seeping through blinds, underwater
green, pond green where turtles emerge
with algae dripping and spring frogs
sing like a machine. Even the machines
are green—the hulking typewriter,
a primitive calculator on its own
green cart. He is a swimmer as he
navigates the aroma of carbon
paper and siftings of cigarette ash,
kicks his feet to draw closer
to the rolling chair covered in green
where he remembers his father
grinning at him from behind columns
of numbers that wave now
like water plants, where everything
except him knows how to breathe.

Overtime for the Dead Letter Detective

Once, almost three decades of mail—Luxor riches—emerged from underpass silt. Damp corners, tea brown stains, back-of-the-closet odor. It took a magnifying glass and cups of black coffee to interpret fading addresses on birthday cards mailed to children long grown, to untangle handwriting of pen pals they remember only when the sky unfolds its flimsy blue aerogramme.

The Brain's Letterbox

The dead letter detective wishes he knew the spot to press when faced with an indecipherable address. He discovers a brain place where reading transpires and adopts the doctor's name for it, begins to see his work as enveloped—first the lost letter, then his decoding brain, each prone to going astray. The detective imagines writing a note from the crease in his left occipito-temporal fissure, a professional memo both empirical and charming in which he rallies the powers of science to his work, but first he must untangle one more envelope's convoluted physiology, decide whether it's worth opening to this daily sensation of loss.

The Dead Letter Detective Writes to His Lover

I will caress your arm beside the water. We will recall the theater while you watch the dog so familiar that I forget. When someone comes around, I will look the other way. When we get home, I will look nowhere but at you. Your slippers, worn at the heel, are dear to my floor. I will breathe into your breath and want only that breathing. When you go, I will write you these letters, haphazardly addressed.

The Dead Letter Detective Uncovers the Address

He slits open the envelope he's squinted at all morning. Like science, he thinks, or math: an equation of penmanship, geography and time. Simple. The detective upholds the regulations, opens no more than he must, reads into the letter only as far as it takes, knows in his bones how much can go amiss with twenty-six letters and ten digits, such a finite set of small signs to stir up all this trouble.

What It Means To Want

The dead letter detective spends most of each year being good. He keeps rules straight, cuffs unsoiled, order he learned from his mother with her tidy hands and smoky perfume. Winter's voluptuous divide—outside colorless and inside glowing—seems more of her method. Each December he handles what the season unloads, letters that make him an expert of other people's catalogs of desires. His own longings aren't simple as a new tie, a moment in someone's presence, the money one simply has coming. In his gray buttonhole he wears a most profligate bloom.

Detective's Holiday

Cottonwoods show their palms
to him in a flicker of breeze

along the Clark Fork, gulping blue:
Crazy Mountains, Beartooth Mountains,

Sapphire Mountains. River so blue
his teeth hurt from glancing, metallic blue,

Bessie blue. He writes a postcard
in a hand he practiced back at his desk,

addresses it to someone in Frenchtown
where dinnertime light burnishes

the silver steeple. He looks up
into the frondy mountain flanks

straining to see the past wearing windy calico,
reeking doeskin. He could swear

a chronicle of footfall, extinction of paw.
Time and distance. Those old two.

The Dead Letter Detective in Spring

I am the official and my business is finding out. No one comes to fetch me from my room with black and gilded letters on the glass. I am only the man who opens other people's mail behind a door marked Official Business. Does it matter that this letter between my fingers is fragile as iris, watercolors dripping from wavering petals? That I inhale its deep purple scent? I tend this paper garden like I would a woman.

The Dead Letter Detective Meets His Match

She didn't mean to unhinge him; it was almost Christmas after all. But where were the parcels she mailed from California—one crate of oranges, an array of silk scarves, the gold compact engraved for her mother? Home from Hollywood where everything is costume, she was barefoot and kept her sunglasses on. He studied his silhouette in each lens, spellbound by the mystery of her undetectable eyes. The fluorescent strip popped overhead and he found he could not locate his hands. She reached for the pen he forgot how to use. He let her finish her parents' address on the form, each letter black and spiked. He wanted a cigarette he had not wanted in years. He wanted music. He wanted the post office to fly so he could explain this intimation of wings.

Detective's Lucid Dream

He wakes mid-dream as morning intervenes. By the time he's drinking tea, last night's drama—a cast of thousands, the connections among them—has flown and church bells ring the early hour. Awake or nearly, he knots his tie and puts out a dish of milk for the stray. His pillow keeps its dent all day, soft cradle, tender bodhisattva, its hollow a gesture he pounds flat each night.

His Métier

Saturdays the dead letter detective checks the fishing gear. He runs his fingers along the old fiberglass rod, yellowing and greening. Light drifts on dustbeams. In the yard crabapples ripen; in the kitchen the only sugar bun sweats and scales on a plate. A calling, writes the priest, is rare and blessed. The detective winds his reel, looks for hooks he inherited from his father. The mail arrives then, and letters slither through the slot toward the stockpile he hoards in the hall.

Deep Afternoon of the Detective

A single set of heel taps, twinned swish of soles, halves of the sharp rhythm of stepping forward. The detective's shadow falls across the floor, separates, then becomes something bright and capable of flight. He watches it go, burnished pocket watch, strawberry sweets, scalloped canopy of a carousel. Goodbye, he thinks. Godspeed. A butterfly in a frame suddenly spotlit by a shaft of afternoon sun blinks. Holds gold, releases it.

Into the Almost

He wearies. The black pocket comb gathers thin silver. Scent of tobacco smoke weaves a gray cocoon. His left hand trembles on the fork clattering against dinner china. He detects odors he remembers emanating from uncles at holidays—alchemy of bourbon and bay rum exhaled from every pore. Old pictures remind him of Sunday afternoons with people he did not understand, and how he has grown to be one more.

The Dead Letter Detective Grows Old

Dead letters! does it not sound like dead men? ... on errands of life, these letters speed to death.
—*Herman Melville*

His life has been a fluency of loss and misdirection. So many orphan letters pulled out of oblivion, their families traced. His failures, tied with string into bundles of one hundred, fold onto office shelves marked each with a year. He is half satisfied. The bundles have dwindled, each year filling less and less of its allotted space. His hand recalls the shape of the cancellation stamp's wooden knob. He will miss its sound daubed onto the inkpad, impressed onto an envelope. Each daily square of the calendar bears the stamped black triangle that means dead.

The Dead Letter Detective Finds a Clue

Leaves outside the window each could turn a lock, even bird feathers, fence pickets, every purple bloom fragrant with marshmallow and a girl's first perfume—watery lavender in a transparent bottle. The detective imagines feeling the click and turn, his fingertips plumb full of nerve. The family dog digs a hole in garden soil, itself another key awaiting a dropped key to sprout a key. All the keys, especially the fat bumblebee, must be tried on tumblers that promise to swing wide the world.

About the Author

Lori Brack's book of poems, *Museum Made of Breath,* was published in 2018 by Spartan Press, Kansas City. The chapbook *A Fine Place to See the Sky* was written as a poetic script for a work of performance art by Ernesto Pujol and published by The Field School in 2010. Her essays and poems have appeared in journals and anthologies including *Rooted: The Best New Arboreal Nonfiction, Another Chicago Magazine, North American Review, The Fourth River, Entropy Magazine, Superstition Review* and its blog, and *Mid-American Review.* She has worked in art centers, libraries, colleges, and for independent artist and education projects.

www.ingramcontent.com/pod-product-compliance
Lightning Source LLC
Chambersburg PA
CBHW071642090426
42738CB00013B/3190